ON THE UNIVERSAL TENDENCY
TO DEBASEMENT IN THE
SPHERE OF LOVE

BY

SIGMUND FREUD

British Library Cataloguing-in-Publication Data
A catalogue record for this book is available from the
British Library

Contents

Sigmund Freud

Sigismund Schlomo Freud was born on 6th May 1856, in the Moravian town of Příbor, now part of the Czech Republic.

Sigmund was the eldest of eight children to Jewish Galician parents, Jacob and Amalia Freud. After Freud's father lost his business as a result of the Panic of 1857, the family were forced to move to Leipzig and then Vienna to avoid poverty. It was in Vienna that the nine-year-old Sigmund enrolled at the Leopoldstädter Kommunal-Realgymnasium before beginning his medical training at the University of Vienna in 1873, at the age of just 17. He studied a variety of subjects, including philosophy, physiology, and zoology, graduating with an MD in 1881.

The following year, Freud began his medical career in Theodor Meynert's psychiatric clinic at the Vienna General Hospital. He worked there until 1886 when he set up in private practice and began specialising in "nervous disorders". In the same year he married Merth Bernays, with whom he had 6 children between 1887 and 1895.

In the period between 1896 and 1901, Freud isolated himself from his colleagues and began work on developing the basics of his psychoanalytic theory. He published *The Interpretation of Dreams*, in 1899, to a lacklustre reception, but continued to produce works such as *The Psychopathology of Everyday Life* (1901) and *Three Essays on the Theory of Sexuality* (1905). He held a weekly meeting at his home known as the "Wednesday Psychological Society" which eventually developed into the Vienna Psycho-Analytic Society. His ideas gained momentum and by the end of the decade his methods were being used internationally by neurologists and psychiatrists.

Freud made a huge and lasting contribution to the field of psychology with many of his methods still being used in modern psychoanalysis. He inspired much discussion on the wealth of theories he produced and the reactions to his works began a century of great psychological investigation.

In 1930 Freud fled Vienna due to rise of Nazism and resided in England until his death from mouth cancer on 23rd September 1939.

ON THE UNIVERSAL TENDENCY TO DEBASEMENT IN THE SPHERE OF LOVE (1912D)

I

If the practising psycho-analyst asks himself on account of what disorder people most often come to him for help, he is bound to reply - disregarding the many forms of anxiety - that it is psychical impotence. This singular disturbance affects men of strongly libidinous natures, and manifests itself in a refusal by the executive organs of sexuality to carry out the sexual act, although before and after they may show themselves to be intact and capable of performing the act, and although a strong psychical inclination to carry it out is present. The first clue to understanding his condition is obtained by the sufferer himself on making the discovery that a failure of this kind only arises when the attempt is made with certain individuals; whereas with others there is never any question of such a failure. He now becomes aware that it is some feature of the sexual object which gives rise to the inhibition of his male potency, and sometimes he reports that he has a feeling of an obstacle inside him, the sensation of a counter-will which successfully interferes with his conscious intention. However, he is unable to guess what this internal obstacle is and what feature of the sexual object brings it into operation. If he has had repeated experience of a failure of this kind, he is likely, by the familiar process of 'erroneous connection', to decide that the recollection of the first occasion evoked the disturbing anxiety-idea and so caused the failure to be repeated each time; while he derives the first occasion itself from some 'accidental' impression.

Psycho-analytic studies of psychical impotence have already been carried out and published by several writers.[1] Every analyst can confirm the explanations provided by them from his own clinical experience. It is in fact a question of the inhibitory influence of certain psychical complexes which are withdrawn from the subject's knowledge. An incestuous fixation on mother or sister, which has never been surmounted, plays a prominent part in this pathogenic material and is its most universal content. In addition there is the influence to be considered of accidental distressing impressions connected with infantile sexual activity, and also those factors which in a general way reduce the libido that is to be directed on to the female sexual object.[2]

When striking cases of psychical impotence are exhaustively investigated by means of psycho-analysis, the following information is obtained about the psychosexual processes at work in them. Here again - as very probably in all neurotic disturbances - the foundation of the disorder is provided by an inhibition in the developmental history of the libido before it assumes the form which we take to be its normal termination. Two currents whose union is necessary to ensure a completely normal attitude in love have, in the cases we are considering, failed to combine. These two may be distinguished as the *affectionate* and the *sensual* current.

The affectionate current is the older of the two. It springs from the earliest years of childhood; it is formed on the basis of the interests of the self-preservative instinct and is directed to the members of the family and those who look after the child. From the very beginning it carries along with it contributions from the sexual instincts - components of erotic interest - which can already be seen more or less clearly even in childhood and in any event are uncovered in neurotics by psycho-analysis later on. It corresponds to *the child's primary object-choice*. We learn in this way that the sexual instincts find their first objects by attaching themselves to the valuations made by the ego-instincts, precisely in the way in which the first sexual satisfactions are experienced in attachment to the bodily functions necessary for the preservation of life. The 'affection' shown by the child's parents and those who look after him, which seldom fails to betray its erotic nature ('the child is an erotic plaything'), does a very great deal to raise the contributions made by erotism to the cathexes of his ego-instincts, and to increase them to an amount which is bound to play a part in his later development, especially when certain other circumstances lend their support.

¹ Steiner (1907), Stekel (1908), Ferenczi (1908).

² Stekel (1908, 191 ff.).

These affectionate fixations of the child persist throughout childhood, and continually carry along with them erotism, which is consequently diverted from its sexual aims. Then at the age of puberty they are joined by the powerful 'sensual' current which no longer mistakes its aims. It never fails, apparently, to follow the earlier paths and to cathect the objects of the primary infantile choice with quotas of libido that are now far stronger. Here, however, it runs up against the obstacles that have been erected in the meantime by the barrier against incest; consequently it will make efforts to pass on from these objects which are unsuitable in reality, and find a way as soon as possible to other, extraneous objects with which a real sexual life may be carried on. These new objects will still be chosen on the model (imago) of the infantile ones, but in the course of time they will attract to themselves the affection that was tied to the earlier ones. A man shall leave his father and his mother - according to the biblical command - and shall cleave unto his wife; affection and sensuality are then united. The greatest intensity of sensual passion will bring with it the highest psychical valuation of the object - this being the normal overvaluation of the sexual object on the part of a man.

Two factors will decide whether this advance in the developmental path of the libido is to fail. First, there is the amount of *frustration in reality*, which opposes the new object-choice and reduces its value for the person concerned. There is after all no point in embarking upon an object-choice if no choice is to be allowed at all or if there is no prospect of being able to choose anything suitable. Secondly, there is the amount of *attraction* which the infantile objects that have to be relinquished are able to exercise, and which is in proportion to the erotic cathexis attaching to them in childhood. If these two factors are sufficiently strong, the general mechanism by which the neuroses are formed comes into operation. The libido turns away from reality, is taken over by imaginative activity (the process of introversion), strengthens the images of the first sexual objects and becomes fixated to them. The obstacle raised against incest, however, compels the libido that has turned to these objects to remain in the unconscious. The masturbatory activity carried out by the sensual current, which is now part of the unconscious, makes its own contribution in strengthening this fixation. Nothing is altered in this state of affairs if the advance which has miscarried in reality is now completed in phantasy, and if in the phantasy-situations that lead to masturbatory satisfaction the original sexual objects are replaced by different ones. As a result of this substitution the phantasies become admissible to consciousness, but no progress is made in the allocation of the libido in reality. In this way it can happen that the whole of a young man's sensuality becomes tied to incestuous objects in the unconscious, or to put it another way, becomes fixated to unconscious incestuous phantasies. The result is then total impotence, which is perhaps further ensured by the simultaneous onset of an actual weakening of the organs that perform the sexual act.

Less severe conditions are required to bring about the state known specifically as psychical impotence. Here the fate of the sensual current must not be that its whole charge has to conceal itself behind the affectionate current; it must have remained sufficiently strong or uninhibited to secure a partial outlet into reality. The sexual activity of such people shows the clearest signs, however, that it has not the whole psychical driving force of the instinct behind it. It is capricious, easily disturbed, often not properly carried out, and not accompanied by much pleasure. But above all it is forced to avoid the affectionate current. A restriction has thus been placed on object-choice. The sensual current that has remained active seeks only objects which do not recall the incestuous figures forbidden to it; if someone makes an impression that might lead to a high psychical estimation of her, this impression does not find an issue in any sensual excitation but in affection which has no erotic effect. The whole sphere of love in such people remains divided in the two directions personified in art as sacred and profane (or animal) love. Where they love they do not desire and where they desire they cannot love. They seek objects which they do not need to love, in order to keep their sensuality away from the objects they love; and, in accordance with the laws of 'complexive sensitiveness' and of the return of the repressed, the strange failure shown in psychical impotence makes its appearance whenever an object which has been chosen with the aim of avoiding incest recalls the prohibited object through some feature, often an inconspicuous one.

The main protective measure against such a disturbance which men have recourse to in this split in their love consists in a psychical *debasement* of the sexual object, the overvaluation that normally attaches to the sexual object being reserved for the incestuous object and its representatives. As soon as the condition of debasement is fulfilled, sensuality can be freely expressed, and important sexual capacities and a high degree of pleasure can develop. There is a further factor which contributes to this result. People in whom there has not been a proper confluence of the affectionate and the sensual currents do not usually show much refinement in their modes of behaviour in love; they have retained perverse sexual aims whose non-fulfilment is felt as a serious loss of pleasure, and whose fulfilment on the other hand seems possible only with a debased and despised sexual object.

We can now understand the motives behind the boy's phantasies mentioned in the first of these 'Contributions' (above, p. 2331), which degrade the mother to the level of a prostitute. They are efforts to bridge the gulf between the two currents in love, at any rate in phantasy, and by debasing the mother to acquire her as an object of sensuality.

2

In the preceding section we have approached the study of psychical impotence from a medico-psychological angle of which the title of this paper gives no indication. It will how ever become clear that this introduction was required by us to provide an approach to our proper subject.

We have reduced psychical impotence to the failure of the affectionate and the sensual currents in love to combine, and this developmental inhibition has in turn been explained as being due to the influences of strong childhood fixations and of later frustration in reality through the intervention of the barrier against incest. There is one principal objection to the theory we advance; it does too much. It explains why certain people suffer from psychical impotence, but it leaves us with the apparent mystery of how others have been able to escape this disorder. Since we must recognize that all the relevant factors known to us - the strong childhood fixation, the incest-barrier and the frustration in the years of development after puberty - are to be found in practically all civilized human beings, we should be justified in expecting psychical impotence to be a universal affliction under civilization and not a disorder confined to some individuals.

It would be easy to escape from this conclusion by pointing to the quantitative factor in the causation of illness - to the greater or lesser extent of the contribution made by the various elements which determine whether a recognizable illness results or not. But although I accept this answer as correct, it is not my intention to make it a reason for rejecting the conclusion itself. On the contrary, I shall put forward the view that psychical impotence is much more widespread than is supposed, and that a certain amount of this behaviour does in fact characterize the love of civilized man.

If the concept of psychical impotence is broadened and is not restricted to failure to perform the act of coitus in circumstances where a desire to obtain pleasure is present and the genital apparatus is intact, we may in the first place add all those men who are described as psychanaesthetic: men who never fail in the act but who carry it out without getting any particular pleasure from it - a state of affairs that is more common than one would think. Psycho-analytic examination of such cases discloses the same aetiological factors as we found in psychical impotence in the narrower sense, without at first arriving at any explanation of the difference between their symptoms. An easily justifiable analogy takes one from these anaesthetic men to the immense number of frigid women; and there is no better way to describe or understand their behaviour in love than by comparing it with the more conspicuous disorder of psychical impotence in men.[1]

[1] I am at the same time very willing to admit that frigidity in women s a complex subject which can also be approached from another angle.

If however we turn our attention not to an extension of the concept of psychical impotence, but to the gradations in its symptomatology, we cannot escape the conclusion that the behaviour in love of men in the civilized world to-day bears the stamp altogether of psychical impotence. There are only a very few educated people in whom the two currents of affection and sensuality have become properly fused; the man almost always feels his respect for the woman acting as a restriction on his sexual activity, and only develops full potency when he is with a debased sexual object; and this in its turn is partly caused by the entrance of perverse components into his sexual aims, which he does not venture to satisfy with a woman he respects. He is assured of complete sexual pleasure only when he can devote himself unreservedly to obtaining satisfaction, which with his well-brought-up wife, for instance, he does not dare to do. This is the source of his need for a debased sexual object, a woman who is ethically inferior, to whom he need attribute no aesthetic scruples, who does not know him in his other social relations and cannot judge him in them. It is to such a woman that he prefers to devote his sexual potency, even when the whole of his affection belongs to a woman of a higher kind. It is possible, too, that the tendency so often observed in men of the highest classes of society to choose a woman of a lower class as a permanent mistress or even as a wife is nothing but a consequence of their need for a debased sexual object, to whom, psychologically, the possibility of complete satisfaction is linked.

I do not hesitate to make the two factors at work in psychical impotence in the strict sense - the factors of intense incestuous fixation in childhood and the frustration by reality in adolescence - responsible, too, for this extremely common characteristic of the love of civilized men. It sounds not only disagreeable but also paradoxical, yet it must nevertheless be said that anyone who is to be really free and happy in love must have surmounted his respect for women and have come to terms with the idea of incest with his mother or sister. Anyone who subjects himself to a serious self-examination on the subject of this requirement will be sure to find that he regards the sexual act basically as something degrading, which defiles and pollutes not only the body. The origin of this low opinion, which he will certainly not willingly acknowledge, must be looked for in the period of his youth in which the sensual current in him was already strongly developed but its satisfaction with an object outside the family was almost as completely prohibited as it was with an incestuous one.

In our civilized world women are under the influence of a similar after-effect of their upbringing, and, in addition, of their reaction to men's behaviour. It is naturally just as unfavourable for a woman if a man approaches her without his full potency as it is if his initial overvaluation of her when he is in love gives place to undervaluation after he has possessed her. In the case of women there is little sign of a need to debase their sexual object. This is no doubt connected with the absence in them as a rule of anything similar to the sexual overvaluation found in men. But their long holding back from sexuality and the lingering of their sensuality in phantasy has another important consequence for them. They are subsequently often unable to undo the connection between sensual activity and the prohibition, and prove to be psychically impotent, that is, frigid, when such activity is at last allowed them. This is the origin of the endeavour made by many women to keep even legitimate relations secret for a while; and of the capacity of other women for normal sensation as soon as the condition of prohibition is re-established by a secret love affair: unfaithful to their husband, they are able to keep a second order of faith with their lover.

The condition of forbiddenness in the erotic life of women is, I think, comparable to the need on the part of men to debase their sexual object. Both are consequences of the long period of delay, which is demanded by education for cultural reasons, between sexual maturity and sexual activity. Both aim at abolishing the psychical impotence that results from the failure of affectionate and sensual impulses to coalesce. That the effect of the same causes should be so different in men and in women may perhaps be traced to another difference in the behaviour of the two sexes. Civilized women do not usually transgress the prohibition on sexual activity in the period during which they have to wait, and thus they acquire the intimate connection between prohibition and sexuality. Men usually break through this prohibition if they can satisfy the condition of debasing the object, and so they carry on this condition into their love in later life.

In view of the strenuous efforts being made in the civilized world to-day to reform sexual life, it will not be superfluous to give a reminder that psycho-analytic research is as remote from tendentiousness as any other kind of research. It has no other end in view than to throw light on things by tracing what is manifest back to what is hidden. It is quite satisfied if reforms make use of its findings to replace what is injurious by something more advantageous; but it cannot predict whether other institutions may not result in other, and perhaps graver, sacrifices.

3

The fact that the curb put upon love by civilization involves a universal tendency to debase sexual objects will perhaps lead us to turn our attention from the object to the instincts themselves. The damage caused by the initial frustration of sexual pleasure is seen in the fact that the freedom later given to that pleasure in marriage does not bring full satisfaction. But at the same time, if sexual freedom is unrestricted from the outset the result is no better. It can easily be shown that the psychical value of erotic needs is reduced as soon as their satisfaction becomes easy. An obstacle is required in order to heighten libido; and where natural resistances to satisfaction have not been sufficient men have at all times erected conventional ones so as to be able to enjoy love. This is true both of individuals and of nations. In times in which there were no difficulties standing in the way of sexual satisfaction, such as perhaps during the decline of the ancient civilizations, love became worthless and life empty, and strong reaction-formations were required to restore indispensable affective values. In this connection it may be claimed that the ascetic current in Christianity created psychical values for love which pagan antiquity was never able to confer on it. This current assumed its greatest importance with the ascetic monks, whose lives were almost entirely occupied with the struggle against libidinal temptation.

One's first inclination is no doubt to trace back the difficulties revealed here to universal characteristics of our organic instincts. It is no doubt also true in general that the psychical importance of an instinct rises in proportion to its frustration. Suppose a number of totally different human beings were all equally exposed to hunger. As their imperative need for food mounted, all the individual differences would disappear and in their place one would see the uniform manifestations of the one unappeased instinct. But is it also true that with the satisfaction of an instinct its psychical value always falls just as sharply? Consider, for example, the relation of a drinker to wine. Is it not true that wine always provides the drinker with the same toxic satisfaction, which in poetry has so often been compared to erotic satisfaction - a comparison acceptable from the scientific point of view as well? Has one ever heard of the drinker being obliged constantly to change his drink because he soon grows tired of keeping to the same one? On the contrary, habit constantly tightens the bond between a man and the kind of wine he drinks. Does one ever hear of a drinker who needs to go to a country where wine is dearer or drinking is prohibited, so that by introducing obstacles he can reinforce the dwindling satisfaction that he obtains? Not at all. If we listen to what our great alcoholics, such as Böcklin,[1] say about their relation to wine, it sounds like the most perfect harmony, a model of a happy marriage. Why is the relation of the lover to his sexual object so very different?

It is my belief that, however strange it may sound, we must reckon with the possibility that something in the nature of the sexual instinct itself is unfavourable to the realization of complete satisfaction. If we consider the long and difficult developmental history of the instinct, two factors immediately spring to mind which might be made responsible for this difficulty Firstly, as a result of the diphasic onset of object-choice, and the interposition of the barrier against incest, the final object of the sexual instinct is never any longer the original object but only a surrogate for it. Psycho-analysis has shown us that when the original object of a wishful impulse has been lost as a result of repression, it is frequently represented by an endless series of substitutive objects none of which, however, brings full satisfaction. This may explain the inconstancy in object-choice, the 'craving for stimulation' which is so often a feature of the love of adults.

[1] Floerke (1902, 16).

Secondly, we know that the sexual instinct is originally divided into a great number of components - or rather, it develops out of them - some of which cannot be taken up into the instinct in its later form, but have at an earlier stage to be suppressed or put to other uses. These are above all the coprophilic instinctual components, which have proved incompatible with our aesthetic standards of culture, probably since, as a result of our adopting an erect gait, we raised our organ of smell from the ground. The same is true of a large portion of the sadistic urges which are a part of erotic life. But all such developmental processes affect only the upper layers of the complex structure. The fundamental processes which produce erotic excitation remain unaltered. The excremental is all too intimately and inseparably bound up with the sexual; the position of the genitals - *inter unrinas et faeces* - remains the decisive and unchangeable factor. One might say here, varying a well-known saying of the great Napoleon: 'Anatomy is destiny.' The genitals themselves have not taken part in the development of the human body in the direction of beauty: they have remained animal, and thus love, too, has remained in essence just as animal as it ever was. The instincts of love are hard to educate; education of them achieves now too much, now too little. What civilization aims at making out of them seems unattainable except at the price of a sensible loss of pleasure; the persistence of the impulses that could not be made use of can be detected in sexual activity in the form of non-satisfaction.

19

Thus we may perhaps be forced to become reconciled to the idea that it is quite impossible to adjust the claims of the sexual instinct to the demands of civilization; that in consequence of its cultural development renunciation and suffering, as well as the danger of extinction in the remotest future, cannot be avoided by the human race. This gloomy prognosis rests, it is true, on the single conjecture that the non-satisfaction that goes with civilization is the necessary consequence of certain peculiarities which the sexual instinct has assumed under the pressure of culture. The very incapacity of the sexual instinct to yield complete satisfaction as soon as it submits to the first demands of civilization becomes the source, however, of the noblest cultural achievements which are brought into being by ever more extensive sublimation of its instinctual components. For what motive would men have for putting sexual instinctual forces to other uses if, by any distribution of those forces, they could obtain fully satisfying pleasure? They would never abandon that pleasure and they would never make any further progress. It seems, therefore, that the irreconcilable difference between the demands of the two instincts - the sexual and the egoistic - has made men capable of ever higher achievements, though subject, it is true, to a constant danger, to which, in the form of neurosis, the weaker are succumbing to-day.

It is not the aim of science either to frighten or to console. But I myself am quite ready to admit that such far-reaching conclusions as those I have drawn should be built on a broader foundation, and that perhaps developments in other directions may enable mankind to correct the results of the developments I have here been considering in isolation.

www.ingramcontent.com/pod-product-compliance
Lightning Source LLC
Chambersburg PA
CBHW021551270326
41930CB00008B/1462